MW01613435

INSIGHT GUIDES

Instant

LONDON

APA PUBLICATIONS

Part of the Langenscheidt Publishing Group

L

CONTENTS

Compiled by Brian Bell
Photography by Apa Archive,
Natasha Babaian, Glyn Genin
Cover photograph:
Telegraph Colour Library

All Rights Reserved
First Edition 2001

As every effort is made to provide accu-
rate information in this publication, we
would appreciate it if readers would call
our attention to any errors that may occur
by communicating with Apa
Publications, PO Box 7910, London SE1
1WE, England. Fax: (44 20) 7403 0290;
e-mail: insight@apaguide.demon.co.uk

Distributed in the UK & Ireland by
GeoCenter International Ltd
The Viables Centre, Harrow Way
Basingstoke, Hampshire RG22 4BJ
Fax: (44 1256) 817-988

Distributed in the United States by
Langenscheidt Publishers, Inc.
46–35 54th Road, Maspeth, NY 11378
Tel: (718) 784-0055. Fax: (718) 784-0640

Worldwide distribution enquiries:
APA Publications GmbH & Co. Verlag KG
Singapore Branch, Singapore
38 Joo Koon Road, Singapore 628990
Tel: (65) 865-1600. Fax: (65) 861-6438

Printed in Singapore by
Insight Print Services (Pte) Ltd
38 Joo Koon Road, Singapore 628990
Tel: (65) 865-1600. Fax: (65) 861-6438

www.insightguides.com

A CITY FOR ALL SEASONS

Londoners like to quote Dr Samuel Johnson, whose influential *Dictionary of the English Language* was published in 1755, as saying: "A man who is tired of London is tired of life." Certainly, Europe's largest city doesn't lack variety, either in its fabric or its culture. Visually, it embraces virtually every form of architecture – not always harmoniously, for Londoners have never been very adept at central planning. As for entertainment, weekly listings magazines bulge with details of shows, exhibitions and events to cater for just about any taste that won't land you in prison. Not for nothing did *Newsweek* magazine dub London "the coolest place on the planet."

Perhaps because the city has spread outwards rather than grown upwards, it has retained a human scale, in its attitudes as much as its edifices. Henry James described it as a "giant animated encyclopaedia with people for pages" – an image that captures the cosmopolitan nature of London's 6.7 million inhabitants.

The Melting Pot

Although in many aspects the epitome of all things British, the capital is also home to people from all corners of the world and it is possible to sample something of their native lifestyle in the areas of London in which they settle, in their communities, and in their cafés and restaurants offering their local food and drink. The capital unites Britain and the rest of the world.

Right: *an image of pomp and pageantry*

Each part of this city has its own distinct atmosphere. There is dignified Westminster, with the government buildings of Whitehall and the Houses of Parliament, the colourful and vibrant West End, a magnet for shoppers and entertainment-seekers, refined Mayfair for the very wealthy, daring Chelsea for the young and artistic.

Observing the City

Other areas include the traditionally bohemian Soho with its nightlife and restaurants; the City, the financial heart of the nation; fashionable Kensington with its world-famous museums; aristocratic Belgravia; intellectual Bloomsbury, home to London University and the British Museum; Holborn and its law courts. The colourful East End has its street markets and immigrant communities and the former Docklands, reborn as a miniature city of high-tech offices and printworks. There's so much to see that, to celebrate the millennium, London constructed the world's largest observation wheel, the London Eye, which stands majestically beside the Thames, the river around which London has been reinventing itself since the Romans first pitched camp here 2,000 years ago.

Endless Possibilities

What to do in London? The possibilities are endless. Have lunch at Fortnum and Mason's on Piccadilly, or take in an open-air performance of Shakespeare in Regent's Park theatre, which you

Above: Big Ben, a famous landmark **Right:** *Leicester Square*

might precede with a cruise along the Regent's Canal. On the South Bank, splash out on a drink at the Oxo Tower, or better still, the restaurants at Shakespeare's reincarnated Globe Theatre or at Tate Modern gallery.

Have a drink at the Grenadier public house on Wilton Row, off Knightsbridge; amble around Harrods; enjoy a meal at the Roof Garden in Derry Street, off Kensington High Street; visit Camden's trendy market on Saturday or Sunday, and earthier Brick Lane market on Sunday. Try a fringe theatre production or a late-night cabaret; stroll through Leicester Square and Covent Garden at night to experience the international flavour of the city. Walk around the City and the East End at the weekend when its offices are closed, and sense the history of the Square Mile from the street names – Crutched Friars, Half Moon Court, Frying Pan, Magpie and Hanging Sword alleys, Knightrider Street and Sermon Lane.

Best of all, just stroll around the centre or take a boat down the Thames. You'll be following in the footsteps of history.

HISTORICAL HIGHLIGHTS

AD43: Londinium settled during second Roman invasion; a bridge is built over the Thames.

61: Boadicca, Queen of the Iceni tribe in East Anglia, sacks the city before being defeated.

410: Troops are withdrawn to defend Rome.

449–527: Jutes, Angles and Saxons arrive in Britain, dividing it into separate kingdoms. Attacks by Vikings.

604: St Paul's Cathedral is founded by King Ethelbert.

c.750: Monastery of St Peter is founded on Thorney Island, to become Westminster Abbey.

8th century: Shipping and manufacturing flourish on the riverbank near today's Strand.

884: London becomes capital under Alfred the Great.

1042: Edward the Confessor moves his court to Westminster and rebuilds the Abbey.

1066: William I, Duke of Normandy and descendant of the Vikings who settled in northern France, conquers Britain and is crowned in Westminster Abbey. The Normans introduce French and the feudal system.

1078: Tower of London's White Tower is built.

1176: A new London Bridge is built of stone.

1191: The City of London elects its first mayor.

1220: St Paul's Cathedral is rebuilt.

1444: Guildhall is rebuilt.

Left: St Paul's Cathedral today

1532: Henry VIII builds Palace of Whitehall, the largest in Europe. It catches fire in 1698.

1534: Henry VIII declares himself head of the Church of England and dissolves the monasteries.

1536: St James's Palace built.

1550: Somerset House is built.

1588: William Shakespeare (1568–1616) begins his dramatic career in London.

1605: Guy Fawkes attempts to blow up Parliament.

1620: The Pilgrim Fathers set sail for America.

1642–49: Civil war between the Cavalier Royalists and the republican Roundheads. The Royalists are defeated. Charles I is executed.

1660: Monarchy is restored under Charles II.

1660–69: Samuel Pepys (1633–1703) writes his diary detailing contemporary events.

1664–66: The Great Plague kills one-fifth of the 500,000 population.

1666: The Great Fire destroys 80 percent of London.

1675: Sir Christopher Wren (1632–1723) starts work on the new St Paul's Cathedral.

1694: The Bank of England is established.

1699: St James's Palace used as a royal court.

1724: St Martin-in-the-Fields is built.

1732: George II makes 10 Downing Street available to Sir

Above: William Shakespeare, England's most famous playwright

Robert Walpole, Britain's first Prime Minister; it is established as the home of future Prime Ministers.

1744: Sotheby's auction house is founded.

1764: The Literary Club is founded by Samuel Johnson, the compiler of first English dictionary.

1783: The country's last public execution is held at Tyburn (now Marble Arch).

1811–20: The Prince Regent, later George IV, gives his name to the Regency style.

1820: Regent's Canal opens.

1824: The National Gallery is established.

1829: Police force is established by Robert Peel.

1834: The Houses of Parliament are built after the Old Palace of Westminster is destroyed by fire.

1837: Buckingham Palace becomes the Sovereign's official residence.

1840s: Trafalgar Square laid out on the site of royal stables to mark Nelson's victory. The British Museum opens.

1851: The Great Exhibition.

1859: A 13-ton bell, Big Ben, is hung in the Clock Tower of the Houses of Parliament.

1863: First section of Underground built between Paddington and Farringdon Street.

1888: Jack the Ripper strikes in Whitechapel.

1890: The first electric railway to be built in deep-level tunnels opens between the City and Stockwell.

1894: Tower Bridge built.

1903: Westminster Cathedral built by the Catholic Church.

Above: Churchill's Cabinet War Rooms *Right:* the British Museum

1909: the Victoria and Albert Museum opens.

1914: World War I begins. First air raids on the city.

1922: British Broadcasting Company transmits first programmes from Savoy Hill.

1939–45: World War II. Children evacuated, London heavily bombed. 29,000 civilians killed and 1.75 million London homes destroyed.

1951: Festival of Britain; new concert halls are built on South Bank near Waterloo.

1956: Clean Air Act is passed.

1976: National Theatre building opened.

1982: Thames Barrier, built to control floods, is completed.

1986: The Greater London Council is abolished.

1991: Canary Wharf, London's tallest building, is completed in the restored Docklands area.

1994: The Channel Tunnel links London with Brussels and Paris.

1996: Shakespeare's Globe, a replica of the original theatre burnt down in 1599, opens on Bankside.

2000: Ken Livingstone becomes London's first elected mayor. Tate Modern gallery opens on Bankside.

PEOPLE AND CULTURE

Saris and sarongs; mosques and mandirs; calypso and chopsticks; turbans and tandooris. Somewhere in London there's something of everything and someone from everywhere. Whereas the nation's non-white population is 4.4 percent, the figure for inner London reaches 20 percent, and more than a quarter of central London's population wasn't born in the UK. Colour is an easy way to tell where someone's family is from; what's less clear is where the many white immigrants have dispersed. The city is a cultural melting pot, which residents tend to take for granted.

City of Immigrants

The first Asian immigrants were resident by 1579. In the 17th century Huguenots – Protestants hounded out of France – settled in Spitalfields in east London where they became silk weavers. In the 19th century the port of London was the largest in the world, and clippers such as the Cutty Sark had races to bring the year's first tea crops home from China. The Chinese community settled in Limehouse, and today there is a flourishing Chinatown around Gerrard Street in Soho.

The traumas of 19th-century Europe led to the mass exodus of Jews, and East London became England's Staten Island, with half a dozen refugee ships arriving every day. The Jews settled

Left: *pouring into London from the suburbs* **Above:** *the Cutty Sark*

around the East End, giving it a dominant character. Since then, the community of around 250,000 has dispersed – to Stamford Hill, Golders Green and Finchley.

The 19th century also brought the railways and a demand for labour. The Irish responded, settling in Camden and Kilburn, north of the rail termini at Euston and King's Cross. Throughout the 20th century the Irish have continued to be a significant force in the building industry. The 256,000 population is scattered today across north and west London.

Ethnic Influences

The 20th century also saw immigration mostly from the Commonwealth, and the resulting ethnic influence extends as far as Heathrow. The airport was largely built by construction workers from India's Punjab.

After the Sikhs came the Caribbeans, who found work on London's buses and Underground railway network. The largest of the non-white ethnic groups are the Indians (689,000), followed by Afro-Caribbeans (500,000), Pakistanis (406,000), Chinese

(122,000), Africans (102,000) and other smaller groups. Today, Britain's Asian population of more than 1 million, including East African Asians, Bangladeshis and Vietnamese boat people, is the largest in Europe.

Disruptions on Cyprus led to immigration in the 1950s and 1960s, with Greek and Turkish Cypriots amicably settling side by side in north London. Today there are 100,000 Cypriots in London – approximately 20 percent of these are Turkish, the same ratio as on the island. The densest Greek community is in Harringay, north London.

In summer, when Middle East temperatures become too hot for comfort, London attracts many Middle Eastern Arabs, who spend much of their time enjoying the coolness of the parks and the breadth of shopping opportunities. The largest Arab communities living in the city are from Egypt, Iraq and Morocco, with a total of around 50,000. Most live in Kensington and Bayswater, and they are very visible in Edgware Road, north of Marble Arch.

Discrimination Matters

While London likes to think of itself as a multi-cultural society, it has very few administrators or top civil servants from what it euphemistically calls the "New Commonwealth". Americans, accustomed to seeing blacks, Hispanics and Amerasians as their

Left: cool interlude **Above:** *multinational Leicester Square*

mayors, state governors, ambassadors to the United Nations, or even presidential contenders, are astonished by the lack of varied races in the higher echelons of Whitehall or other government departments. Their absence is also evident in the City and Inns of Court.

Many blame discrimination, others cite the language barrier, weak academic qualifications, and the relatively advanced age at which the ethnic professionals attain their skills. Until the general election of 1987, there were no ethnic minority members of Parliament; that situation has begun to change.

All the same, London welcomes every type of visitor. Karl Marx and Mahatma Gandhi studied here. Charles de Gaulle lived in exile here. Writers such as Paul Theroux, Salman Rushdie and V.S. Naipaul chose to work here. People from every corner have settled here, and people from all over the world come to visit. Even Harrods, the quintessentially English store, has been owned by an Egyptian since 1985, and it sells 40 per cent of its merchandise to tourists.

London Icons

The Cockney

Being a cockney is as much a state of mind as it is a turn of phrase, and it is not exclusively genetic. The original definition of a cockney – someone born within the sound of Bow bells, the clarion of St Mary-le-Bow in Cheapside in the City – would today exclude most Londoners. The resident population of the City (London's financial area) is tiny, and the sound does not penetrate far.

Above: *the 'City of London' is the financial district*

Cockneys no longer need to be white and Anglo-Saxon; there are Italian, West Indian, Jewish and Pakistani cockneys. What they share are certain traditions, being a member of an identifiable urban group, a distinctive language – and a quick sense of humour.

They are concentrated in the East End of London, and are popularly portrayed on the television soap, *EastEnders*. News vendors and market traders are often cockneys – shrewd, street-wise people, who prefer to work for themselves and tend to value freedom more than wealth. The aristocracy of the cockneys are the pearly kings and queens, whose suits are embroidered with mother-of-pearl buttons.

Cockney is a London accent, widely broadcast by 'Enry 'Iggins in the musical *My Fair Lady*. It has no use of the aspirant "h", the "t" in the middle of words such as "butter", or the final "g" in words ending "ing". Cockneys traditionally speak in a rhyming slang which supposedly originated among barrow boys who didn't want their customers to understand what they said to each other. A "whistle" is a suit, short for whistle and flute, "north and south" means mouth, "trouble and strife" means wife.

The Bobby

Britain's bobbies, unlike most cities' police forces, have an avuncular image. They seldom carry guns (nor, when balloted, do they indicate any desire to do so) nor do they wear dark glasses. Somewhere within their clothing are a truncheon (baton), a puny

Above: read all about it in London's Evening Standard

whistle and a pair of handcuffs. This lack of personal arsenal reflects the fact that London is a relatively safe metropolis.

A low annual murder rate of around 200 in the metropolitan area was helped by a ban, in 1997, on the possession of hand guns. Minor assaults are the most common felony. Oxford Circus Underground station is a black spot for pickpockets, and bag snatchers. Bag snatchers also operate in busy pubs in the West End and the centre of town.

Today there are more than 28,000 officers in the Metropolitan police department (the Met). The force was started in 1829 when the old watchmen were abolished by the Home Secretary, Sir Robert Peel, who gave his name to the force, first as "Peelers", then as "Bobbies".

The Cabbie

Taxi drivers, or cabbies, are true Londoners. They are experts on London, and are essential to its life, coursing through the city's veins in their little black cells. (Not that all the cabs are black any more: advertising has turned some of them into garish perambulating billboards.)

Would-be drivers must register with the Public Carriage Office and then spend up to four years learning London in minute detail (a process called "doing the Knowledge"). They do this by travelling the streets of the metropolis on a moped, whatever the weather, working out a multitude of routes from a clipboard mounted on the handlebars. Once qualified, the London cabbie

Above: London bobbies in force in the West End

is his (or, occasionally, her) own boss, a condition that spells heaven to many British people.

About 20,000 taxi drivers work in London, of which half are owner-drivers. The others either hire vehicles from the big fleets or work night shifts in someone else's cab. In all, there are more than 15,000 vehicles in service. Each driver and each cab is licensed by the Public Carriage Office, and there are strict regulations controlling both. A driver is obliged to take a passenger wherever he wishes to go within the Metropolitan Police District or City of London, provided the journey doesn't exceed 6 miles (10 km). He is also obliged to go by the most direct route in distance and/or time.

Taxi driving in London is still very much a male profession. Only a small proportion of drivers are women, though the number is rapidly increasing. It is also very much a white, working-class occupation, and traditionally a large percentage of drivers are Jewish (which can make it hard to find a cab on Jewish New Year).

Most London taxi drivers, particularly the older ones, love

Above: *taxi cabs queue for custom*

to talk. Parodying the notice in most cabs that reads: "Thank you for not smoking", a cartoon in the satirical magazine *Private Eye* amended it to read: "Thank you for not interrupting".

The Double Decker

The red double-decker bus is to London what the cable car is to San Francisco, or the gondola to Venice. It's part of the fabric of the city. But it's rather more than that: in the form of the traditional Routemaster, it is a mechanical miracle, introduced in 1959 with an expected lifespan of 17 years and still on the road. Of 2,825 originally built, 900 are going strong.

They've been threatened with the scrap heap many times. In 1970 London Transport decided to phase out conductors. This meant phasing in pay-as-you enter buses with driver-operated doors, thus eliminating the joys of hopping on and off the platform of a passing vehicle and of chatting with the conductor.

In 1996 the European Union pronounced that the open platforms were dangerous and that London's Routemasters should be abolished on the grounds of instability. In a bid to prove their safety, London Transport staff filled the top deck of a bus that was then cornered at a tilt of 40 degrees. It didn't topple over.

Above: room on top **Right:** *"Les Mis", a long-running success*

Entertainment

Theatreland

London's theatrical history goes back to a playhouse opened at Shoreditch in 1576 by James Burbage, the son of a carpenter and travelling player. In modern times, live theatre was supposed to succumb first to movies, then to television, yet it is still one of those essential attractions that every visitor is supposed to experience. It remains a mystery, however, what cultural sustenance coachloads of foreign tourists derive from a convoluted Alan Ayckbourn farce or an imaginative production of Shakespeare set in a variant of the Third Reich. More cautious visitors play it safe and opt for one of the blockbuster musicals.

Shrewd theatrical brains realised that revenue from musicals could be used to underwrite more serious work. In particular, Trevor Nunn, who grew rich by directing several of Lloyd Webber's musicals, including *Cats*, masterminded the Royal Shakespeare Company's 1985 production of *Les Misérables*. Despite a tepid critical welcome, "Les Mis" went on to conquer the world, and Nunn became director of the Royal National Theatre.

Traditionalists claimed that the mania for musicals was squeezing out new drama productions. Yet a glance at the theatre listings in *Time Out* magazine doesn't entirely bear out this claim. Classics continue to be staged at the Royal National Theatre and the Barbican, new writing is still put on at the Royal Court and the Bush, experimental work and alternative comedy are mounted at the fringe theatres, and playwrights such as David Hare, Tom Stoppard and Terry Johnson do not lack an audience. What's more, favourite thespians such as Alan Bates, Michael Gambon, Ian McKellan, Maggie Smith, Diana Rigg and Judi Dench can virtually guarantee to attract a full house. Recently, Hollywood stars such as Kevin Spacey and Nicole Kidman have taken stage roles in London, pulling in the crowds.

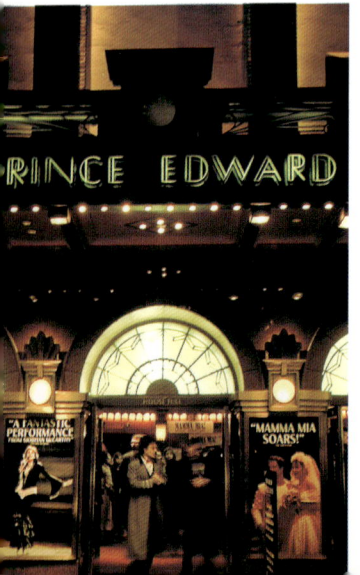

In addition to the 50 central theatres, there are around 60 recognised fringe venues in the capital, including the Young Vic (in The Cut, near the Old Vic), the Almeida (in Islington) and the Half Moon (in the East End). In the summer there is open-air theatre in Regent's Park (usually Shakespeare).

One of the most important features of London theatre is the presence within it of two major subsidised companies: the Royal National Theatre and the Royal Shakespeare Company, both of

Left: *lights, action, music*

which seem to stagger from one financial crisis to the next. In terms of audiences, both are successful and originate many productions that transfer into the mainstream theatre of the West End. The National, on the South Bank, is the more congenial building, despite its intimidating concrete exterior, and has three auditoria. The Barbican, which is the RSC's London home for part of the year (its main base is Stratford-upon-Avon), opened in 1982 and has a splendid and comfortable main auditorium, but the bars and concourses are impersonal. It also has a small-scale auditorium.

Great Restaurants

London is one of the great culinary cities of the world. This is partly due to the breadth of cosmopolitan cuisines available and also the fact that there has been a re-evaluation of the indigenous cuisine of the British. Its once scorned reputation of badly cooked, unimaginative, stodgy meals has been overturned by the

Above: *a fashionable place to eat*

new generation of innovative modern-minded British chefs. They have injected new life into traditional English recipes, indeed rediscovering many, by combining them with French and ethnic influences. They now take pride in making the best of top quality and seasonal ingredients whilst also making meals lighter. For example, dishes such as "roast best end of lamb with two sauces of lime and coriander, yoghurt and mint" (Wilson's) or "courgette flowers with lobster mousseline and a caviar butter sauce" (Sutherlands).

The traditional English practices of Sunday lunch, roast carveries, and fish and chips are still very much part of the scene and sampling them provides an insight into everyday life in England. However, choose carefully, as there is a huge difference between good and bad versions of these meals. Even the 1996 "mad cow disease" scare didn't entirely kill demand for roast beef – although some chefs tactfully found other European sources for their meat.

The main concentration of London's restaurants are to be found in the West End, with Soho providing the most interesting and widest choice, whilst Covent Garden offers good value pre-theatre suppers. The City, meanwhile, with its oyster bars and restaurants traditionally catering for the business luncher, becomes a ghost town in the evenings and at weekends.

Above: *a much-loved British staple*

Although London's restaurants are expensive by many people's standards, reflecting the high cost of living, eating out in this capital has arguably never been so good. Ethnic restaurants – especially Indian – provide some of the best value meals in town, whereas pubs and wine bars often provide good inexpensive snacks in surroundings that are preferable to a fast food hamburger joint. And for a really cheap meal you can't go far wrong with a take-away of good old British fish and chips.

London's Pubs

Like most other things in a city this size, it is impossible to generalise about the 5,438 pubs in London. Some have live music, some stage striptease, some are genteel and some rough, many are Victorian (a strange product of such a morally critical age) and some were opened last week, perhaps part of a chain such as The Slug and Lettuce – commerce is no respecter of traditional names. Most Londoners have a favourite, the choice of which depends as much on the people that frequent it as on the decor.

London has several pubs that date from the 17th century, and many retain the atmosphere of that era. One of the best examples is The George in Southwark, the only original galleried coaching inn in London. Rebuilt in 1676, it has remained

Right: *welcoming sign in Southwark*

largely unchanged and it is now owned by the National Trust. The galleries were once the entrance to the inn's rooms. A fine example of the explosion of pubs during the Victorian era (known for their engraved mirrors, grand central bars and dark velvet upholstery) is the Duke of Cumberland in Fulham, where such decor is completed by Grecian urns.

The traditional drink in a pub is English beer (ale or bitter). The genuine article is drawn up by hand pump and served at the temperature of the cellar; chilling literally kills it, as beer continues to ferment in the barrel. There are many more types of beer on sale than you will find in a Continental brasserie or Bierkeller and a drinker who asks for "a pint of beer" will be asked to be more specific. A lager is closest to Continental and American beers, a stout is a dark, strong beer, but most seasoned British

drinkers drink bitter, a light brown beer that should taste fresh, hoppy, with no fizzy gas and is never chilled but served at room temperature.

A pint is just over half a litre and many people order a "half", instead of a full pint. In traditional pubs, the customer orders his or her drink at the bar and pays for it immediately. It is not necessary to tip but some regular drinkers offer to buy the bar staff a drink.

Most pubs in London consist of more than one room and almost certainly have more than one entrance, dating from the days when pubs had a public bar and a

Above: the George is the only galleried coaching inn left in London

separate lounge, which was more comfortably furnished and carpeted. This tradition has all but died out. Chains such as All Bar One and the Slug and Lettuce are a growing presence in London. These light, airy, fashionably furnished pub/bars are especially accessible to single drinkers, women and anyone wanting a quiet drink during the daytime. Many of them also offer their customers imaginative modern menus.

Most traditional pubs also serve food, although probably not all day. A sign outside that says "pub grub" generally refers to food bought over the bar rather than an elaborate restaurant-style meal. In London the menus available at lunchtime generally provide good value and often include traditional British dishes. Bangers and mash (sausages and mashed potato, often accompanied by fried onions), bubble and squeak (a mixture of fried cabbage, onions and potato, often served with cold meat), Ploughman's lunch (Cheddar cheese, bread and mixed pickles), steak and kidney pie or pudding, and sausage rolls are all traditional pub fare, although many pubs now offer a more adventurous selection of food, with Mediterranean influences.

Above: *al fresco refreshment*

A–Z OF LONDON

British Museum

The British Museum, on Great Russell Street, is a treasure house of more than 6½ million objects. Collections from the Ancient World dominate – notably the Elgin Marbles as well as numerous other Greek and Roman exhibits and an exceptional collection of Egyptian antiquities – but almost every period of human history is represented.

When the British Library ceased to share the same building in 1997, the museum glassed over the Great Court, the area around the library's Reading Room in the centre of the building, to create the largest covered public square in Europe. The mix of styles – the ultra hi-tech glass panelling of the new roof set against the sturdy, measured classicism of the original 19th-century building – is striking, and a new multimedia visitor centre makes the museum more accessible for more than 6 million visitors a year. A few highlights give an impression of its vast scope.

Greece and Rome: The highlight for most visitors is the Elgin Marbles, more correctly known as the Parthenon Sculptures, which decorated the mid-5th-century BC temple to Athena in Athens. The sculptures were brought to Britain in 1801 by Lord Elgin, then British ambassador to Constantinople, and the Greek authorities have since maintained that Elgin exported them illegally and have campaigned strenuously for their return.

Ancient Egypt: The gilded coffin of Henutmehyt, dating from 1290 BC, is beautiful, and there is also a mummy of a cat. The Rosetta Stone, the Egyptian tablet from the 2nd century BC, provided the key to reading ancient Egyptian hieroglyphics.

Left: the courtyard of the British Museum

Ancient Near East: Clay tablets contain cuneiform inscriptions, one of the oldest forms of writing. One, nearly 5,000 years old, records the delivery of barley to a temple. A plastered skull from Jericho is around 9,000 years old.

The Orient: Those with a taste for Ming vases will find it more than satisfied. The Japanese collections, though not as ancient, contain wall hangings, furniture, masks, ceramics of all kinds, lacquer work and jade.

The Americas: There are a number of hugely impressive Olmec statues and other works from around 1000 BC as well as magnificent carved Mayan slabs from the 8th century AD. The rather later Aztec artefacts are equally striking.

Early Europe: For many visitors, a highlight of the museum is Lindow Man, a 2,000-year-old Briton whose body was preserved largely intact in a peat bog and discovered only in 1978. Among the elaborate Celtic artefacts are shields, coins, and a wide variety of jewellery and drinking vessels.

Medieval Europe: The Sutton Hoo treasure consists of objects unearthed in 1939 from the grave of a 7th-century Anglo-Saxon king. Other medieval objects include the 7th-century illuminated Lindisfarne Gospels, an intricately patterned 12th-century gilt cross from Germany, a striking example of the high levels of craftmanship in the so-called Dark Ages and a 7th-century chess set whose lumpy, helmeted figures, their faces set in curious scowls, are strangely beautiful.

www.thebritishmuseum.ac.uk

Left: *one of the museum's 6½ million objects*

Buckingham Palace

This has been the main London home of the royal family since Queen Victoria moved here in 1837. Her grandfather, George IV, employed John Nash to enlarge the building, which had been built in the 17th century for a Duke of Buckingham. Nash added two wings, later enclosed in a quadrangle, and its main facade was designed by Aston Webb in 1913.

The State Rooms are open to the public for a few weeks in late summer when the Queen is away. These include the Dining Room, Music Room, White Drawing Room and Throne Room, where there are paintings by Vermeer, Rubens and Rembrandt. The tour also allows a glimpse of the 40-acre (16-hectare) Palace Gardens where the celebrated garden parties are held. Guests are invited because of some worthy contribution made to the nation, but few of the 8,000 people a year get to shake the Queen's hand.

The Queen has one of the greatest private art collections in the world – including an exceptional collection of Leonardo da Vinci drawings – and the one-room gallery has had changing exhi-

Above: Buckingham Palace viewed from St James's Park

bitions since it opened in 1952, yet some still remain unseen. The adjoining Royal Mews contain royal vehicles, from coaches to Rolls-Royces. The Gold State Coach, built for George III in 1762, is still used by the Queen on major state occasions.

The Queen and the Duke of Edinburgh occupy about 12 of the palace's 650 rooms, on the first floor of the north wing, overlooking Green Park. If the Queen is in residence, the royal standard flies from the centre flagpole. On great occasions the family appears on the first-floor balcony to wave to the crowds.

Most of the everyday crowds come to see the Changing of the Guard at 11.30 every morning (alternate mornings in winter) outside the palace. The New Guard, which marches up from Wellington Barracks, meets the Old Guard in the forecourt of the palace and they exchange symbolic keys to the accompaniment of regimental music. The Irish Guards are distinctive for their bearskin hats (now made from synthetic materials). Behind the scenes are more sophisticated protection measures: there is a large nuclear shelter underneath the palace.
www.buckingham-palace.co.uk

Canary Wharf

The Canary Wharf complex, London's tallest building, dominates the massive office developments in London's former Dock-

Above: part of the Canary Wharf complex

lands. It is centred on Cesar Pelli's 800-ft (244-metre) tower, set down on a massive man-made island in the middle of the West India docks. If one approaches on the Docklands Light Railway, it seems like a bustling modern terminal, with shops and offices leading immediately from the station, and a sudden business-like air. Several national newspapers are based in Canary Wharf.

Covent Garden

Named after a convent whose fields occupied the site, Covent Garden was for centuries the principal market for vegetables, fruit and flowers, and the workplace of Eliza Doolittle, the flower girl in George Bernard Shaw's *Pygmalion* who later burst into song as *My Fair Lady*. The market moved out in 1974 and, since the early 1980s, the area has seen a transformation that has become a blueprint for turning old commercial buildings into a mall of shops and stalls. Numerous restaurants and cafés, shops

Above: *browsing among the stalls in Covent Garden*

and showrooms occupy the old warehouses in the narrow streets and alleyways surrounding the market square. There is a good line in street entertainers who are part of the establishment. Would-be performers must undergo rigorous auditions, ensuring standards are kept high.

The main piazza was originally laid out with colonnaded town houses designed by Inigo Jones around 1630, and inspired by the 16th-century Italian architect Andrea Palladio. A small market was established here as early as 1661. The terraces and arcades have long since disappeared, although the arcade on the north side, where the Rock Garden dispenses equal help-

ings of American-style hamburgers and live rock music, has been recast. Many of the streets around Covent Garden have been cordoned off with pedestrian pathways.

The portico of St Paul's, the actors' church, used as a backdrop in *My Fair Lady* and also designed by Inigo Jones, dominates the western end of the square, on to which it turns its back. The vaults and grounds of this church are said to contain the remains of more famous people than any other church except Westminster Abbey, although the headstones have long been removed. An annual clowns' service is held here.

The old flower market, in the southeastern corner of the square, is now home to the London Transport Museum, which has a big collection of horse-drawn coaches, buses, trams, trains, rail carriages, and some working displays. Next door to the London

Above: *Covent Garden is a magnet for the young*

Transport Museum, but entered from Russell Street, is the Theatre Museum, which contains portraits, costumes, stage sets and much memorabilia.

Greenwich

This Thameside district in southeast London houses Sir Christopher Wren's Old Royal Observatory, where Greenwich Mean Time was established in 1884. It has Britain's largest refracting telescope, and a fine display of time-keeping ephemera, including John Harrison's famous clocks whose story was told in Dava Sobel's 1995 book *Longitude*. A brass rule on the ground marks the dividing line between the Eastern and Western hemispheres, making it possible to have a foot in both worlds. It's a steep climb to the observatory, but the views are great.

The National Maritime Museum has been redeveloped to create 16 new galleries around a spectacular courtyard spanned

Above: enjoying the views at Greenwich

by the largest glazed roof in Europe. It traces the history both of the Royal Navy and the Merchant Navy, as well as the colonisers and discoverers. There are primitive coracles and glittering royal barges and memorabilia include the tunic worn by Lord Nelson at the Battle of Trafalgar in 1805, with the hole made by the bullet which killed him; the battle itself is replayed with computer-generated realism.

In dry dock on the waterfront is the record-breaking *Cutty Sark*, a tea-clipper that used to race to be the first to bring the new season's tea from China. Dwarfed by it is the tiny *Gypsy Moth IV*, in which Sir Francis Chichester sailed single-handed around the world in 1966–67.

The superbly proportioned Royal Naval College was built in two halves to leave the view from Queen's House to the river. Queen's House, further back in the park, was a gift to Anne of Denmark from her husband, James I, designed by Inigo Jones, though not completed until 1637, in Charles I's reign. This was

Above: the prow of the Cutty Sark

the first building in England to be designed entirely in the Classical style. It has a well-restored 17th-century interior.

Designed by Wren, Hawksmoor and Vanbrugh, with gardens laid out by Le Nôtre, it was built as a hospital for naval pensioners to match Wren's Royal Hospital in Chelsea. The highly decorated chapel is open to the public, as is the Painted Hall, an astonishing piece of work which took the artist, Sir James Thornhill, 18 years to paint. The highly decorated chapel, restored in rococo style after a fire in 1779, hosts concerts and recitals as well as services. On display in Queen Mary's Court are the Crown Jewels of the Millennium, a splendid collection of authentically recreated crown and state jewels from around the world. The copies were commissioned for posterity at the end of the 19th century by the historian P.J. McCullagh when he realised that monarchies were collapsing all over Europe

Harrods

Presiding over fashionable Knightsbridge is Harrods , the most famous department store in Britian. The well-stocked food hall is decorated with art nouveau tiles and mosaics. The store was started by Henry Charles Harrod as a grocery business in 1849, although the present building was opened in 1905. The store's boast used to be that there was noth-

ing in the world it could not obtain for you. An elephant, sir? No problem. The business is now owned by the Egyptian Al-Fayed family, who bought it in 1983. *www.harrods.com*

Right: a famous name in retailing

HMS Belfast

Moored near Tower Bridge, this is Britain's only surviving example of the big-gun armoured warships built during the first half of the 20th century. Now part of the Imperial War Museum, the *Belfast* gives a fascinating insight into the work of a warship and into the strains of life on board. Launched in Belfast in 1938, it was in active service until 1965, and served in World War II and Korea. At the height of its career, it accommodated 950 men.

www.iwm.org.uk/belfast.htm

Houses of Parliament

The clock tower of the Houses of Parliament has become a symbol of the city. Its elaborately fretted stone sides rise nearly 330 ft (100 metres) to a richly gilded spire above the clock and a 13-ton hour bell supposedly nicknamed Big Ben after a rather fat government official called Sir Benjamin Hall who was commissioner of works when the bell was installed.

The oldest part of the Houses of Parliament is Westminster Hall, begun in 1078. The thick buttressed walls are spanned with a magnificent hammer-beamed oak roof. Among those condemned to death here were Sir Thomas More, who fell foul of King Henry VIII; King Charles I, accused of treason against Parliament; and the 17th-century revolutionary Guy Fawkes, who tried to blow up the buildings.

Above: HMS Belfast **Right:** *the Houses of Parliament*

In 1835 a fire achieved what Guy Fawkes had failed to do and most of the ancient rambling Palace of Westminster was destroyed. Westminster Hall and a small crypt chapel survived. Parliament took the opportunity to build a comfortable purpose-built meeting place. The present Houses of Parliament were created in an exuberant Gothic style by Sir Charles Barry and Augustus Pugin. The immense Victoria Tower marks the southern end of the building, and the grand entrance to the House of Lords. A Union Flag (the national flag, colloquially called the Union Jack) flies from the tower when parliament is in session. Night sittings are indicated by a light shining over the clock tower.

The building covers 8 acres (3.2 hectares); there are 11 open courtyards and more than 1,100 rooms. Apart from the ceremonial state rooms and the two main debating chambers, the House of Lords and the House of Commons, there are libraries, dining rooms, tea rooms and offices. Many of the walls are covered with heroic Victorian paintings and the woodwork is carved in an intricate Gothic fashion. Anyone can watch debates from the visitors' gallery. *www.parliament.uk*

Hyde Park

When combined with the adjacent Kensington Gardens, Hyde Park is London's largest park. The *Domesday Book* of 1086 records that the park was then inhabited by wild bulls and boars. It was first owned by the monks of Westminster Abbey, and after ecclesiastic property had been confiscated in the Reformation, Henry VIII turned it into a royal hunting ground. It was opened to the public in the 17th century.

The Serpentine, which attracts hardy swimmers all year round at the lido, was created in the 1730s as a royal boating pond, and boats can still be hired from the north bank. Harriet Westbrook, the first wife of the poet Shelley, drowned herself here in 1816. William III's Route du Roi (Rotten Row) is where the well-heeled canter their horses in the morning.

At the northeast corner of the park, near Marble Arch, is Speaker's Corner, where anyone can legally pull up a soap box and sound off on Sunday afternoons – a tradition going back to the days of the Tyburn gallows, when condemned men were allowed to have a last word.

Imperial War Museum

The Imperial War Museum, south of the river near Waterloo railway station, is housed in the 1811 Bethlehem hospital for the insane – the name was corrupted to "Bedlam" and passed into the English language. The museum has a social conscience, and there is much civilian material from the two world wars as well as the latest in modern weaponry. There's a recreation of a wartime air raid on a London street, and visitors can effectively experience the sights, smells and sounds in the trenches during World War I.

Over the past 10 years, the museum has expanded its remit from the purely military to include a rolling programme of exhibitions on many aspects of modern history, often only loosely connected with conflict – from code breaking and refugees to fashion and sport.

A new floor houses a permanent Holocaust exhibition. It is built around the testimonies of a selection of survivors who tell of their experiences chronologically from the origins of anti-Semitism through to its horrific conclusion. Film footage accompanies the stories, as does rare and important historical material, some of it lent by former concentration camps in eastern Europe. Larger items include a section of a deportation railcar, the entrance to a gas chamber, a dissection table, shoes collected from victims of the gas chambers and a large model of part of Auschwitz. *www.iwm.org.uk*

Left: *a summer's day in Hyde Park* **Above:** *the Imperial War Museum*

Kew Gardens

Kew, in the western suburbs of London, is synonymous with the Royal Botanic Gardens. The 300-acre (120-hectare) gardens were established in 1759 with the help of Joseph Banks, the botanist who named Botany Bay on Captain James Cook's first voyage to Australia. Other explorers and amateur enthusiasts added their specimens over the centuries, making this a formidable repository and research centre. The gardens are also very beautiful, with grand glasshouses, including the Palm House and Waterlily House, Orangery, mock Chinese pagoda, and the Dutch House, a former royal palace. George III was locked up here when it was thought that he had gone mad. His wife Charlotte had a thatched summerhouse built in the grounds as a picnic spot. There are also two small art galleries of horticultural subjects. *www.rbgkew.org.uk*

London Aquarium

Situated in the old County Hall building on the South Bank between Waterloo and Westminster bridges, the London Aquarium offers seven different aquatic environments on three levels.

It begins with freshwater stream, represents the world's great oceans and ends with coral reefs, rainforest and mangrove swamps. Thousands of specimens representing 350 species of fish inhabit over 440,000 gallons (2 million litres) of mains-fed but specially treated water. Atmospheric sounds, smells and lighting have been employed to great effect: dragonflies hum around the freshwater stream, and tropical birds call in the steamy rainforest.

Slicing through two floors of the complex are two giant 25-ft (7.6-metre) high cylinders representing the Atlantic and Pacific oceans, the latter patrolled by three different types of shark that weave through models of the monolithic statues found at Easter Island. Ledges allow spectators to sit within a window's-breadth of these mean-looking creatures; the windows are made of acrylic and are 17 times stronger than ordinary glass. *www.londonaquarium.co.uk*

London Dungeon

Nestling by London Bridge, the London Dungeon concentrates on the macabre. Bloodcurdling screams issue from mechanical waxwork figures, an executioner garrottes some pathetic soul, while another vomits blood into an overflowing barrel. There's a tour of Jack the Ripper's East End of London, and a simulation of the Great Fire of 1666 encourages visitors to run for their life through a maze of hot corridors, arriving at a rotating tunnel with a kaleidoscopic array of fiery colours. The London Dungeon is one of the capital's most popular attractions. *www.thedungeons.com*

Left: *for fabulous fish* **Above:** *welcome to the London Dungeon*

London Eye

Towering over the Thames across from the Houses of Parliament is the British Airways-sponsored London Eye, the world's largest observation wheel, built to mark the millennium. At 450 ft (135 metres), it is the fourth highest structure in London and is supported on one side only, like a giant desktop fan. The hub and

spindle weigh 330 ton – heavier than 40 double-decker buses. The 32 fully enclosed capsules, each holding 25 people, take 30 minutes to make a full rotation – a speed slow enough to allow passengers to step in and out of the capsules while the wheel keeps moving. On a clear day, views stretch for 25 miles (40 km).

So stately is the rotation that there is no feeling of movement inside the capsules. A solid floor keeps vertigo at bay and a central bench is provided in case anyone feels dizzy. Londoners will enjoy spotting familiar sites, but visitors may be left with an impression of a low-rise urban sprawl with only a few sights immediately identifiable. *www.british-airways.com/londoneye*

London Zoo

Located in Regent's Park *(see separate entry)*, the zoo has more than 8,000 animals. The Penguin Pool by the Russian architect, Berthold Lubetkin, and the

Left: the London Eye

Aviary by Lord Snowdon are of architectural interest. The animals can be handled in the children's enclosure. The Web of Life Exhibition, a glass pavilion, celebrates the variety of biological diversity. *www.londonzoo.co.uk*

Madame Tussaud's

In an age when computer animation routinely fills cinema screens with the miraculous, what impels 7,000 people a day to stand in line breathing in the traffic fumes of London's Marylebone Road in order to gaze at mute, immobile effigies with glass-fibre bodies and wax heads? Knowing the answer to that question has turned Madame Tussaud's into the city's top tourist attraction, beating the Tower into second place.

A key ingredient in the success is that the models are no longer roped off or protected by glass cases. You can stroll right up to them – an impertinence their bodyguards would never permit in real life. You can give Saddam Hussein a piece of your mind. You can be photographed with your arm around a Hollywood idol.

The story began during the French Revolution in 1789 when Marie Grosholtz, trained by a doctor in modelling anatomical subjects in wax, was asked to prepare death masks of famous victims of the guillotine. Although she married a French engineer,

Above: the Fab Four in Madame Tussaud's

François Tussaud, in 1795, she left him in 1802 to spend the next 33 years touring Britain with a growing collection of wax figures. Today those gory beginnings are echoed in the waxworks' Chamber of Horrors, which contains the blade that sliced off Marie Antoinette's head and re-creates various tableaux of torture. Vlad the Impaler acts as doorman.

www.madame.tussauds.com

Millennium Bridge

This innovative suspension bridge, linking St Paul's Cathedral on the north side of the Thames with the Tate Modern gallery on the south, became in 2000 the first new river crossing in central London since 1894. The slender design – resembling a giant stainless-steel scalpel – won praise, but opening-day crowds caused the bridge to sway excessively, and it had to be closed after two days for a major engineering rethink.

National Gallery

Overlooking Trafalgar Square on the north side is the imposing neoclassical facade of the National Gallery, designed by William Wilkins in 1838 with an additional modern wing by Robert Venturi completed in 1991. This is the country's most important art gallery and is home to works of the great British and European artists such as Gainsborough, Rembrandt, Rubens,

Above: *the Millennium Bridge* ***Right:*** *the National Gallery*

El Greco, Vermeer and Van Gogh. Nearly all the European painting movements are represented by the 4,500 works, including some dating from the 13th century. *www.nationalgallery.org.uk*

National Portrait Gallery

This famous collection, in St Martin's Place behind the National Gallery, has more than 4,500 portraits of the nation's most illustrious men and women by its most esteemed artists, such as Joshua Reynolds and John Constable, and photographers. It includes the only known portrait of Shakespeare to be painted while he was alive. *www.npg.org.uk*

Natural History Museum

One in a group of world-class museums in South Kensington, the Natural History Museum, built between 1873 and 1880, is an imposing neo-Gothic pile with a grand central hall. The Life Galleries have exhibits on early humans, Darwin's theory of evolution, human biology, birth and whales (including a life-size

model of a blue whale), but undoubtedly the biggest draw is the Dinosaur Gallery: for many years the star of the dinosaurs was an 85-ft (26-metre) diplodocus skeleton in the museum's central hall, but in 2001 a new life-size animatronic Tyrannosaurus Rex stole the show.

In the New Earth Galleries, an escalator rises through a slowly rotating model of the globe, giving the sensation that you are turning, not the globe. You can also experience a simulated earthquake in a Japanese supermarket, complete with sound effects. *www.nhm.ac.uk*

Notting Hill

This lively area in west London – one in which several races and just about every social class rub shoulders – leapt to stardom in the 1999 movie *Notting Hill*, in which a Hollywood star, Julia Roberts, found love with a local bookseller, Hugh Grant. But the area had long been celebrated for the Notting Hill

Carnival, a massive three-day Caribbean festival that takes place over the area in the last weekend of August, with children's parades on the Sunday and adults' parades on Monday. It was started in 1966 in an attempt to unite the local communities after race riots in the streets the previous year. Months of work go into the costumes worn by the dancers in the procession, which features Trinidadian steel bands and attracts 750,000 onlookers and 10,000 police officers. It's a joyous occasion, but many feel it has outgrown the area and should be relocated to somewhere like Hyde Park.

Oxford Street

Oxford Street, an old Roman road, was once known as Tyburn Street and the condemned were transported along this street to the gallows from Newgate prison or the Tower of London. Watching crowds produced a ready clientele for shopkeepers.

The first department stores were built here – one of the finest, Selfridges, by Gordon Selfridge, a Chicago millionaire. His store opened in 1909, though the present American neoclassical emporium wasn't completed until 1926. It had 130 departments, a roof garden and an ice-cream soda fountain. Marks & Spencer, the drapers, opened their largest store in Oxford Street in 1930. The stretch of street east of Oxford Circus is less upscale in its retailing ambitions. *www.oxfordstreet.co.uk*

Left: the Notting Hill Carnival in action **Above:** Oxford Street

Piccadilly Circus

This is the heart of London's entertainments centre, the place where the first illuminated signs appeared in 1890. A few years later the statue of Eros, Greek god of love, was erected as the Angel of Charity in honour of the philanthropic Seventh Earl of Shaftesbury (1801–85) who drove the broad thoroughfare which bears his name through the squalid slums that had grown up to the northeast.

Adding to Piccadilly's bright lights are the refurbished Criterion Theatre on the south side, and a former music hall, the London Pavilion, on the east. This now contains the high-tech Pepsi Trocadero Centre, whose varied attractions include a Segaworld games center; an IMAX cinema; and Rock Circus, where you can see a variety of not especially lifelike pop stars in waxwork, and hear their songs.

Above: Eros presides over Piccadilly Circus

Portobello Road Market

Built on the site of a pig farm named after an English victory over Spain at Porto Bello in the Gulf of Mexico in 1739, Portobello Road in west London has developed over the past 50 years into a major antiques market. By far the busiest time is on Saturday mornings, when the street fills with stalls. Traders claim to be local characters but are much sharper than they may seem, and the only certain bargain is the lively atmosphere.

River Thames

London grew up around Old Father Thames, a highway that decisively shaped its landscape, history and geography. The British navy at its height built ships in the great naval yards of Deptford, Woolwich and Chatham, and trained its officers in Sir Christopher Wren's magnificent buildings at Greenwich. Between 1860 and 1900, when London reaped the harvest of the British Empire and its docklands were the warehouse of the world, the river became the dark and poverty-stricken highway described by Charles Dickens, where the most wretched of Londoners scavenged for flotsam and jetsam in the mud.

Given such a background, the best way of making sense of this complex metropolis is to take a trip on the river. The journey upstream from Westminster pier to Hampton Court takes

Right: on the Thames

around three hours. Downstream through the City and Docklands to Greenwich from Charing Cross pier takes about an hour. It is not necessary to go both ways by boat. The main line railway serves both Hampton Court and Greenwich and the foot tunnel beneath the Thames at Greenwich leads to Island Gardens on the Isle of Dogs, the last stop on this branch of the Docklands Light Railway.

Regent's Park

North of Marylebone Road, behind Madame Tussaud's waxworks, is Regent's Park, an elegant 470-acre (190-hectare) space sur-rounded by John Nash's handsome Regency terraces. The gardens are formally planted, notably the roses in Queen Mary's Garden at the heart of the Inner Circle and not far from the Open Air Theatre where Shakespeare's plays are staged in summer. The boating lake is a tranquil spot, and Regent's Canal runs through the north of the park. A big attraction is London Zoo (see page 42). On the northwest side of the park is Lord's Cricket Ground, headquarters of the English game.

Royal Academy

On the north side of Piccadilly is Burlington House, the home of the Royal Academy of Arts, where painters such as Reynolds, Constable, Turner and Millais either studied or taught. Its sum-

*Above: boating in Regent's Park **Right:** the Royal Albert Hall*

mer exhibition, to which anyone may submit work, usually generates controversy. At other times the Academy mounts high-profile exhibitions – often outstanding – to raise funds to help maintain its art school. The building itself entombs part of the Earl of Burlington's town house built in the 1660s, and occasional access can be had to a fine suite of rooms. *www.royalacademy.org.uk*

Royal Albert Hall

This striking circular building, facing Kensington Gardens to the north, is a huge, ornate structure with a capacity of 8,000. It measures 272ft by 238ft (83 by 73 metres), the glass and iron dome is 135ft (41 metres) high internally, and the 150-ton organ has 10,000 pipes. The frieze around the outside illustrates "The Triumph of Arts and Sciences". It was built in 1870 and much of the necessary money was raised by selling off in perpetuity 1,300 of its seats, many of which are still owned privately.

Every July the Henry Wood Promenade Concerts, a series of classical concerts where the promenading audience have the

option of standing or sitting on the floor, provide a rich diet of music. The televised Last Night of the Proms has something of the atmosphere of a football match, and the crowd's shouts make use of the hall's famous echo. The echo prompted a traditional joke that the hall is the only place where a British composer can be sure to hear his work twice.

The hall is named after Queen Victoria's German husband, Prince Albert, and in Kensington Gardens opposite the hall is the Albert Memorial . Badly eroded by pollution, it was expensively restored to its former gilded glory in the 1990s.
www.royalalberthall.com

Royal Opera House

Just in time to mark the millennium, the Royal Opera House opened its doors in December 1999 after a £120 million refurbishment that had closed it for 18 months. Before the renovations, the politics behind the beautiful facade in Covent Garden had been vicious and the backstage facilities cramped. After the reopening, the politics seemed more benign and singers, dancers and musicians all had more space in which to rehearse and prepare for performances. Audiences at last benefited from air conditioning.

On the outside, Inigo Jones's piazza was completed, with colonnades running all the way round this corner of the piazza. Beneath them were two arcades and an entrance from the market square. For the first time the Royal Ballet Company now has a base at the Opera House,

Above: seated bronze outside the Royal Opera House

with six ballet studios and a performance studio seating 200. A further performance space, a 400-seat Studio Theatre, enables the two companies to give around 100 performances here a year.

The highest priced venue in London, the Opera House has had to contend with unimpressed audiences: price riots were common in the 19th century, and in 1809 lasted 61 nights. An effort is now being made to make a greater number of less expensive tickets available, but administrators continue to complain that opera in London in grossly underfunded.
www.royalopera.org

St Paul's Cathedral

Rising majestically above the wartime smoke, miraculously unharmed, was the magnificent dome of St Paul's Cathedral. The first purpose-built Protestant cathedral is Sir Christopher Wren's greatest work. A tablet above Wren's plain marble tomb reads:

Above: *the interior of St Paul's Cathedral*

Lector, si monumentum requiris, circumspice, "Reader, if you wish to see his memorial, look around you."

Historians believe that the first church on the St Paul's site was built in the 7th century, although it only really came into its own as Old St Paul's in the 14th century, and by the 16th century it was the tallest cathedral in England. Much of the building was

destroyed in the Great Fire of 1666. Construction on the new St Paul's Cathedral began in 1675, when Wren was 43.

The architect was an old man of 78 when his son Christopher finally laid the highest stone of the lantern on the central cupola in 1710. In total, the cathedral cost £747,954 to build, and most of the money was raised through taxing coal arriving in the port of London. The building is massive and the Portland stone dome alone weighs more than 50,000 tons. Generations of schoolchildren have giggled secret messages in St Paul's Whispering Gallery, more than 100 ft (30 metres) of perfect acoustics. *www.stpauls.com*

Science Museum

The Science Museum is part of South Kensington's trio of instructive museums (the others are the Natural History Museum, *see page 45,* and the Victoria & Albert Museum, *see page 63*). It traces the history of inventions from the first steam train – Stephenson's Rocket – to the battered command module from

Above: mesmerised by science at the Science Museum

the Apollo 10 space mission. There are a number of working models on the seven floors of exhibition space which encompass computing, medicine, photography, chemistry and physics. The vast Wellcome Wing has lots of hands-on displays plus (for an extra charge) an IMAX cinema and flight simulators. There are imaginative exhibits on genes and the future of digital communications. *www.sciencemuseum.org.uk*

Shakespeare's Globe

Shakespeare's Globe, on the south bank of the Thames between Blackfriars and Southwark bridges, is a re-creation, completed in 1997, of the original theatre in which William Shakespeare (1564–1616) acted and was a part-owner. *Hamlet*, *Othello*, *King Lear* and *Macbeth* all had their first performances at the Globe. The season of the open-air galleried theatre runs from May to September, and the actors are encouraged to interact with the

Above: *the Globe Theatre*

audience. No amplification is needed because the acoustics are so good that a whisper can be clearly heard in the galleries, and only natural lighting is used. The theatre can accommodate 1,500 people – 600 standing and the rest seated. The wooden benches can feel distinctly hard by Act III, but you can rent cushions.

The fascinating Shakespeare's Globe Exhibition, adjacent to the theatre, aims to bring aspects of Shakespeare's work vividly to life using modern technology and traditional crafts. *www.shakespeares.globe.org*

Soho

This area has always been popular with immigrants. Flemish weavers, French Huguenots, Greeks, Italians, Belgians, Maltese, Swiss, Chinese and Russian Jews have sought refuge here. Their influence is still felt in the patisseries, delicatessens, restaurants and shops. Four hundred years ago Soho was an area of open fields,

Above: *Berwick Street Market in Soho*

and its name is said to come from a hunting cry: "So-ho, so-ho!".

Today the area is the heart of London's nightlife with dozens of clubs, cabarets and strip clubs and the capital's main gay quarter. By day the cosmopolitan atmosphere is more obvious. Chinese, Indian, Arabic, Spanish and Italian restaurants abound and the streets throng with people from all over the world. Having acquired a reputation for sleaziness, the area was cleaned up in the 1980s. In the 1960s the now legendary Carnaby Street became the focal point for a popular youth culture. These days it lives on its reputation and has become a tourist attraction in its own right.

Tate Britain

Located between Vauxhall and Lambeth bridges, this gallery, founded in 1897 by Henry Tate, of the Tate & Lyle sugar empire, is the storehouse for the Tate's collection of British art from 1500 to the present day. Works are shown in a series of thematic displays, with historical and contemporary pieces exhibited side by side. Among the outstanding British paintings are portraits by Thomas Gainsborough (1727–88), evocative views of the English countryside by John Constable (1776–1837) and intensely dramatic and impressionistic seascapes and landscapes by the prolific J.M.W. Turner (1775–1851). Notable contemporary British artists represented include Howard Hodgkin, Damien Hirst and Mona Hatoum.

www.tate.org.uk/britain

Right: *Tate Britain*

Tate Modern

In 2000 the Tate boldly moved its entire international modern collection and part of its contemporary collection, most of which had been kept in storage for lack of space, from its old gallery at Millbank to the converted Bankside Power Station on the south side of the Thames.

This vast edifice, incorporating some 4.2 million bricks and topped with a 325-ft (99-metre) high chimney, competes for attention with the remarkable contents of its 88 galleries, which range from Picasso's *Weeping Woman* and Dalí's *Lobster Telephone* to the very latest works of international artists.

Visitors enter through the Turbine Hall, the old boiler room – an impressive space covering more than 35,000 sq. ft (3,300 sq. metres) and rising six storeys. Now devoid of its power-generating machinery, the hall is capable of housing massive sculptural works and installations.

Along the north side of the Turbine Hall are the main rooms of the gallery. The permanent collection, including work by Picasso, Matisse, Mondrian, Duchamp, Dalí, Bacon, Pollock, Rothko and Warhol, plus sculpture by Giacometti, Hepworth and Epstein, is on the third and fifth levels. Works are organised in four themes – the nude, landscape, still life and history painting. Displays are multi-disciplinary, enabling installations, sculptural works and photography to be interspersed among the paintings.

Above: the Turbine Hall at Tate Modern

Although this thematic system of display has been criticised by those who prefer a more traditional chronological system of hanging, Tate Modern's curators argue that the themes chosen are "classic" ones, rooted in genres originally established by the French Academy. The intention is that the juxtaposition of work produced before the 1970s (an imprecise dividing point) with the work of contemporary artists will help visitors to understand how artists have learnt from one another since 1900. *www.tate.org.uk/modern*

Tower Bridge

This is one of London's most distinctive and frequently photographed landmarks. In the 19th century, a time of great industrial expansion, there was a pressing need to improve circulation over the river without hindering the access of ships into Lon-

Above: *Tower Bridge, a triumph of Victorian engineering*

don's docks. The result was this triumph of Victorian engineering, constructed between 1886 and 1894. A steel frame is held together with 3 million rivets, clad with decorative stonework in High Gothic style. The central section of the bridge opens around 500 times a year to let large ships pass through; it takes 90 seconds for the bascules to lift fully.

The Tower Bridge Experience, an associated exhibition and tour, gives visitors the chance to see most of the inside of the bridge: down in the basement, inside the two turrets and along the raised walkways, from where on a clear day there is a spectacular view of London. The highlight on the walkways is a collection of old photographs showing the building work of the bridge in progress. *www.towerbridge.org.uk*

Tower of London

Encircled by a moat (now dry), with 22 towers and standing at the edge of the medieval City walls by Tower Bridge, the Tower of London is Britain's finest medieval military monument. Uniquely, it served as a fort, arsenal, palace and prison. It was also the treasury, record office, observatory, royal mint and zoo,

Above: the Tower of London is steeped in royal history

as animals given to monarchs were, until 1834, kept in the Lion Tower by the present entrance.

The Tower was a royal palace until the mid-16th century, and the main palace buildings were above Traitors Gate, the river entrance through which prisoners were brought. Henry VI and Richard II were among royal prisoners, while Edward IV's heirs, Prince Edward, aged 12, and Prince Richard, 10, were murdered in the Bloody Tower in 1483. The executioner's axe came down on Tower Hill, but the privileged lost their lives on the block inside the Tower's grounds, among them two wives of Henry VIII: Anne Boleyn and Catherine Howard. In World War II German spies were shot here.

At its centre is the White Tower built by William I after his conquest of England in 1066 and containing the fine Norman Chapel of St John on the first floor. Henry VIII added the domestic architecture of the Queen's House behind the Tower on the left, which is where the Tower's governor lives. The most recent buildings are the 19th-century Museum and Waterloo Barracks, next to the Tower, which contains the Jewel House where the Crown Jewels are a major attraction. There are a dozen crowns and a glittering array of swords, sceptres and orbs used on royal occasions. Many date from Charles II's reign (1660–85), when the monarchy was restored.

Forty Yeomen Warders, attired in Tudor uniforms, live in the Tower. They first took up their posts under Edward VI (1547–53). Their nickname, Beefeaters, may come from the French buffetier, a servant, though an "eater" was also used

Right: a Beefeater poses

to describe a servant in English. The raven is the symbol of the Tower. Nine live here, looked after by The Ravenmaster, a Yeoman Warder. It is said that the day the ravens leave the Tower, England will fall. As a precaution, their wings have been clipped. *www.tower-of-london.com*

Trafalgar Square

This monumental space, designed by John Nash, vividly reflects Britain at the height of its power, when its navy was invincible and it ruled more than a quarter of the planet. At the centre of the square is the 167-ft (50-metre) Corinthian column and 12-ft (3.6-metre) statue of Horatio Nelson, the admiral who defeated Napoleon Bonaparte at the Battle of Trafalgar in 1805. The four handsome lions (1847) are by Edwin Landseer and around

Above: Trafalgar Square

the square Canada House, South Africa House and Uganda House are memories of distant Empire days. The square has long been the site of public gatherings, political demonstrations and New Year celebrations.

There is a rumour that the French crown jewels are buried beneath the square, placed there by Madame du Barry, mistress of Louis XV, when the site was part of the old royal mews. Every Christmas a 70-ft (20-metre) Norwegian spruce is erected in the square, a gift from the city of Oslo in recognition of the protection given to the Norwegian royal family in World War II.

Victoria & Albert Museum

The greatest of the group of museums around South Kensington is undoubtedly the Victoria and Albert Museum in Cromwell Road, which Henry Cole began assembling the year after the Great Exhibition, though Queen Victoria did not lay the foundation stone of the current building until 1899, 38 years after Albert died. Its 1909 facade is by Aston Webb, who put the front on Buckingham Palace. Inside is the world's richest and most diverse collection of decorative arts and it is impossible on one visit to see all the vast halls and galleries that cover six floors.

There are extraordinary collections of sculpture, pottery, china, engravings, illustrations, metalwork, paintings, textiles, period costumes and furniture. All are genuine, even colossal plaster-cast copies and the admitted forgeries and fakes. The Chinese, Japanese and Islamic rooms are splendid. Highly recommended is a visit to the Morris, Gamble and Poynter rooms, leading

Right: statue of David in the V&A

from the Italian Renaissance rooms on the ground floor. These spectacular Arts and Crafts designed rooms, with stained glass, Minton tiles and a flourish of appropriate quotations, were the museum's original refreshment rooms.

There is also a Frank Lloyd Wright room, a print collection, a selection of European paintings (including a John Constable collection) and a shop. *www.vam.ac.uk*

Wallace Collection

Housed in an imposing 18th-century townhouse in Manchester Square, behind Oxford Street, this is a rich and beautifully laid out museum containing paintings by Titian, Valázquez, Rembrandt, Rubens, Canaletto, Hals, Poussin and Bonington, a good collection of 18th-century French paintings (Fragonard, Watteau) plus fine furniture and porcelain. *www.wallace-collection.org.uk*

Westminster Abbey

The most historic religious building in Britain is Westminster Abbey. It is also an outstanding piece of Gothic architecture, which is probably more striking for the intricate detail on the inside than from its relatively plain outward aspects. Much of the present abbey, the third on the site, was built in the 13th-century in early English Gothic-style by Henry III. During the 16th century, Henry VII added on the remarkable chapel at the eastern

Above: the V&A is a celebration of decorative arts

end of the sanctuary in the late Gothic Perpendicular style. During the 18th century, Nicholas Hawksmoor designed the distinctive towers at the main west entrance.

Until the 16th century the abbey was an important monastery. In addition to their religious duties, the monks translated and copied important books and manuscripts. They also ran a school to teach reading and writing in English and Latin, starting a long tradition of quality formal education in Britain. Henry VIII dissolved the monasteries in 1534 when he quarrelled with the Pope but Westminster Abbey continued to be used as the royal church for coronations and burials. All but two of the reigning monarchs from William the Conqueror onwards were crowned here.

The Abbey has always had a special place in the life of the nation because of its royal connections. So many eminent figures have been honoured in this national shrine that extensive areas of the interior have the cluttered and confused appearance of an overcrowded sculpture museum. The Tomb of the Unknown Warrior houses the body of a soldier brought back from France after World War I,

Right: Westminster Abbey

along with the soil for the grave, as an anonymous representative of the countless dead.

Poets' Corner lies beyond the nave in the south transept. Geoffrey Chaucer was the first poet to be buried here, in 1400. Other literary figures here include Alfred Lord Tennyson; the poet and dramatist Ben Jonson, who is buried standing upright; William Shakespeare, John Milton, John Keats and Oscar Wilde. Countless other literary luminaries have only monuments. Behind the sanctuary are magnificent and ornate royal chapels and tombs. The Chapel of Edward the Confessor is the earliest, containing the tomb of the founder of the abbey himself, and that of Henry III, the man who rebuilt it in its present form.

The Abbey also houses the English Coronation Chair, built in 1300 for Edward I and still used for the installation of new monarchs. One of the most refined and daring pieces of late Gothic architecture is the Chapel of Henry VII. With carved stalls, brilliantly patterned banners and exquisite fan-vaulting on the

Above: the facade of Westminster Abbey

roof, this is a breathtaking sight. Looking at its apparently delicate structure, it is difficult to believe that it withstood the blast of a bomb dropped nearby during World War II.
www.westminsterabbey.org.uk

Westminster Cathedral

Sometimes confused with Westminster Abbey, this is London's foremost Roman Catholic church. Situated on Victoria Street, close to Victoria railway station, it has bold red-and-white brickwork which makes it look like a gigantic layer cake. Built at the end of the 19th century on the site of a prison, it was designed by John Bentley in outlandish Italian-Byzantine style not seen elsewhere in London. The cathedral has a 330-ft (100-metre) striped tower incorporating a lift for public use. Views from the gallery at the top are superb.

The interior of the cathedral is spacious and sumptuously decorated, with many of the chapels enriched with coloured marble cladding on the walls. Among the highlights are the richly decorated Lady Chapel with mosaics by Robert Anning Bell, and the Stations of the Cross designed by Eric Gill. Cathedral treasures include St Thomas Becket's mitre.

Right: *Westminster Cathedral*

ESSENTIAL INFORMATION

The Place

Situation 51.30°N 0.10°W, on the same latitude as the Kamchatka peninsula in Pacific Russia and the north tip of Newfoundland, Canada. The capital of the United Kingdom is on the River Thames 40 miles (64km) from the North Sea.

Population 6.4 million, 9 million in the larger metropolitan area.

Area 610 sq miles (1,580 sq km).

Religion Protestant (Church of England): the monarch is the titular head of the church; the primate is the Archbishop of Canterbury, whose London address is Lambeth Palace.

Currency pounds, divided into 100 pence (depending on exchange rate, £1 is approximately US$1.44–$1.50).

Weights & Measures officially metric, though imperial is still used, notably for distances (miles) and beer (pints).

Electricity 220 volts. Square, three-pin plugs, unique to Britain and some old British Empire countries; two-pin shaver plugs.

Time Zone Greenwich Mean Time (GMT), 1 hour behind Continental European Time and 5 hours ahead of Eastern Seaboard Time. Summer time (+ 1 hour) from March to September.

Direct dialling From abroad, dial 44 + 20, then an 8-digit number. Internally, codes are not needed.

The Climate

The English are justly famous for their preoccupation with the weather, a fascination that is largely due to its unpredictable nature. The climate in London is mild, with the warming effects of the city itself keeping off the worst of the cold in winter.

Left: London calling – traditional red telephone boxes

Snow and temperatures below freezing are unusual, with January temperatures averaging 43°F/6°C. Temperatures in the summer months average 64°F/18°C, but they can soar, causing the city to become airlessly hot (air-conditioning is not universal). However, temperatures can fluctuate considerably from day to day and surprise showers catch people unawares all year round. *For recorded weather information, tel: 0891-500 401.*

Government

When people refer to London, they mean the county of Greater London. When they speak of the City of London, they generally mean the financial district, the historic square mile between St Paul's Cathedral and the Tower of London, governed by the Corporation of London and headed by the Lord Mayor, which even has its own police force. The rest of the metropolis is run by 12 inner boroughs and 20 outer boroughs, each of which is responsible for local services.

After the Conservative prime minister Margaret Thatcher abolished the Labour-leaning Greater London Council (GLC) in the 1980s, London was for 15 years the only major European city without a coordinating government – and this showed, for example, in poorly funded public transport. In May 1998 a referen-

Above: bearing the emblem of the City of London

dum was held, and Londoners voted in favour of a new governing body and an elected mayor of the entire city. Ken Livingstone, a former leader of the GLC, became the first mayor.

The Economy

In the 19th century London was the largest city in the world. Now its economy is almost entirely financial and service-based, with tourism playing a huge part. Its manufacturing industries and shipping have moved out, accounting for the 20 percent drop in population.

Public Holidays

January New Year's Day (1)
March/April Good Friday, Easter Monday
May May Day (first Monday), Spring Bank Holiday (the last Monday in the month)
August Summer Bank Holiday (last Monday in the month)
December Christmas Day (25), Boxing Day (26)

Getting There

BY AIR

London is served by two major international airports: Heathrow, 15 miles (24 km) to the west (mainly scheduled flights); and Gatwick, 24 miles (40 km) to the south (scheduled and charter flights), with the smaller air-

Right: a great way to sightsee

ports of Stansted and Luton to the north of London. There is also the tiny London City Airport situated in Docklands, a few miles east from the City, used by small aircraft connecting London with European cities.

CHANNEL TUNNEL

The Channel Tunnel provides Eurostar passenger services by rail from Paris Nord (3 hours) and Brussels Midi (2 hours 40 minutes) to London's Waterloo. UK Eurostar bookings, tel: 0990 186 186; for bookings in the UK from abroad, tel: (44) 1233-617 775. In the US call 1-800-EUROSTAR or 1-800 356 66711.

Vehicles are carried by train through the tunnel to Folkestone in Kent from Nord-Pas de Calais in France by Le Shuttle. Bookings are not essential, but advisable at peak times. Fares vary according to the time of travel: late at night or in the early morning is much cheaper. Enquiries in France: 33 1-49 70 01 75 and in the UK: 0990 353 535.

BY FERRY

Sea services operate between 12 British and over 20 Continental ports. The major ferries have full facilities and for people arriving by boat there is a sense of occasion that can never be matched by an underground train. The shortest ferry crossing time from the Continent is about one hour 30 minutes, from Calais to Dover.

Brittany Ferries (UK tel: 0990 360 360) sails to Portsmouth

***Above:** Waterloo Station, gateway to London from the Continent*

from St Malo (33-2 99 82 80 80) and Caen (33-2 31 36 36 36); to Poole in Dorset from Cherbourg (33-2 33 88 44 44); and to Plymouth from Roscoff (33 2 98 29 28 00) and St Malo depending on season. They also sail from the port of Santander in northwest Spain (34-4 222 0000).

P&O Stena Line (www.posl.com; UK tel: 0990 980980) sails to Dover from Calais (33-3 21 46 04 40); Portsmouth from Cherbourg and Le Havre (33-2 35 19 78 50); Newhaven from and to Dieppe. Services also run from Bilbao in Spain to Portsmouth. Seafrance (UK tel: 0870 571 1711) operates a ferry service from Calais to Dover; P&O North Sea Ferries (www.ponsf.com; UK tel: 01482 311 177) runs from Zeebrugge to Hull.

Entry Regulations

VISAS AND PASSPORTS

To enter the United Kingdom, you need a valid passport (or any form of official identification if you are a citizen of the EU). Commonwealth citizens, Americans, EU nationals or citizens of most other European and South American countries do not require visas.

Above: *fast and reliable, but not particularly cheap*

Health

If you fall ill and are an EU national, you are entitled to free medical treatment for illnesses arising while in the UK. Many other countries also have reciprocal arrangements for free treatment. However, most visitors will be liable for medical and dental treatment and should ensure they take out adequate health insurance in advance of their stay.

In the case of minor accidents, your hotel will know the location of the nearest hospital with a casualty department.

Money

Most banks open between 9.30am and 4.30pm Monday–Friday, with Saturday morning banking common in shopping areas. Major English banks tend to offer similar exchange rates; it's only worth shopping around if you have large amounts of money to change. Banks charge no commission on sterling traveller's cheques. If a London bank is affiliated to your own bank, it will make no charge for cheques in other currencies either; but there will be a charge for changing cash into another currency. International credit cards are widely accepted.

Some High Street travel agents, such as Thomas Cook, operate bureaux de change at comparable rates. There are also private bureaux de change (some are open 24 hours), but be sure to check their rates carefully: these can be very low while commissions are often high.

Above: many London hospitals are centres of excellence

Media

Print: Britain has an immensely diversified press, with 10 national daily newspapers and 10 national Sunday newspapers. London's main newspaper, the *Evening Standard*, comes out Monday–Friday from late morning. The top listings magazine is the long-established weekly *Time Out*, but the *Evening Standard* includes a good (and free) listings magazine, *Hot Tickets*, on Thursdays. Foreign newspapers and magazines can be found at many street newsstands and at mainline stations.

Television: Britain has a reputation for fine broadcasting. There are five national terrestrial channels: BBC1 and BBC2 without advertising, plus three commercial channels, ITV, Channel 4, and Channel 5. There are more than 60 cable and satellite channels. Pricier hotels will often have a choice of cable stations such as CNN or NBC's Super Channel.

Radio: The BBC has a strong line-up of stations, notably Radio 4 (news and documentaries) and Radio 3 (classical music). In addition, there's a wide range of commercial stations.

Security and Crime

London, long known for its unarmed police force, is still a comparatively safe place for tourists. The main problem, as in any metropolis, is petty theft, and skilled teams of pickpockets do well on the Underground railway system, in shopping streets and in bars and restaurants.

Right: what's on at the NFT

Accommodation

London hotel prices are higher than in any other major city in Europe – and you don't necessarily get much for your money. Some budget accommodation is simply appalling, and many more expensive hotels are dull and unmemorable.

In the peak seasons (Christmas, Easter and April to September), book well in advance. The London Tourist Board provides an accommodation booking service through its information centres or by phone (credit or debit cards only): tel: 020-7604 2890. At less busy times of the year, many hotels offer discounted weekend rates.

B&Bs offer an alternative to impersonal hotels, where you stay as a paying guest in a private home. The London Bed & Breakfast Agency (tel: 020-7586 2768) has some 200 homes on its books, with prices from around £40–80 for a double room per night. Uptown Reservations (tel: 020-7351 3445) has a smaller, more upmarket selection: double rooms with private bath cost £85.

Above: the entrance to the Savoy Hotel on the Strand

London has seven youth hostels run by the Youth Hostel Association. Beds in dormitories cost about £16–22 a night (tel: 01727-855215). A good independent hostel is the Generator (tel: 020-7388 7666), on Compton Place in Bloomsbury. Its prices are normally higher than in YHAS, but you don't share with strangers.

Tourist information

The British Tourist Authority has offices worldwide. Visit *www.visitbritain.com* or write to Thames Tower, Black's Road, London W6 8EL to request information.

Australia: Level 16, Gateway, 1 Macquarie Place, Sydney, NSW 2000. Tel: 02-9377 4400. Fax: 02-9377 4499.

Canada: Suite 120, 5915 Airport Road, Mississauga, Ontario, L4V1T1. Tel: (905) 405 1840. Fax: (905) 405 1835.

New Zealand: 3rd Floor, Dilworth Building, Queen/Customs Street, Auckland 1. Tel: 9-303 1446. Fax: 9-377 6965.

Singapore: Cecil Court, 138 Cecil Street, Singapore 069 538. Tel: 65-227 5400. Fax: 65-227 5411.

South Africa: Lancaster Gate, Hyde Lane, Hyde Park, Sandton 2196. Tel: 11-325 0342. Fax: 11-325 0344.

USA – Chicago: 625 N. Michigan Avenue, Suite 1510, Chicago, IL 60611-1977. Tel: (312) 787-0464. Fax: (312) 787-9641.

USA – Los Angeles: 11661 San Vicentre Blvd, Los Angeles, CA 90049. Tel: (310) 820-4206. Fax: (310) 820-4406.

Above: sights of interest are well signposted

USA – New York: 7th Floor, 551 Fifth Avenue, New York, NY 10176-0799. Tel: (212) 986-2266. Fax: (212) 986-1188.

Useful websites

www.a-london-guide.co.uk Virtual London. Filled with information on events, tourist attractions, hotels and theatre.

www.thisislondon.com This site, maintained by the *Evening Standard* newspaper, has detailed listings of events in the city.

www.londontown.com Run by the London Tourist Board and Convention Bureau, the site is well designed and has information on maps, hotels, accommodation, restaurants, pubs and all attractions. Worth consulting before a trip or even a night out.

www.netlondon.com Internet directory. Includes links to hotels, museums, theatres and (if you are so inclined) Prince William.

www.londonnet.co.uk An online magazine style guide to London. Features cover certain aspects of travel but its more a resource for news and entertainment information.

london.hotelguide.net A website detailing all levels of London accommodation.

www.londononline.co.uk Provides up-to-date going-out information for the city. More trendy than traditional.

www.smoothhound.co.uk/london.html A good listing of the less expensive end of London's accommodation.

ww.travelbritain.com/london/tourism A basic site for basic travel information for the tourist avoiding complications.

Above: *a familiar beacon*

And now for the big picture…

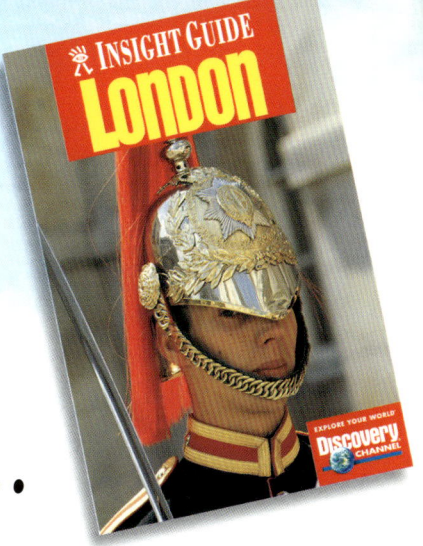

The text you have been reading is extracted from *Insight Guide: London*, one of 200 titles in the award-winning Insight Guides series. Its 310 pages are packed with expert essays covering London's history and culture, detailed itineraries for the entire city, a comprehensive listings section, a full set of clear, cross-referenced maps, and hundreds of great photographs. It's an inspiring background read, an invaluable on-the-spot companion, and a superb souvenir of a visit. Available from all good bookshops.

Also from Insight Guides…

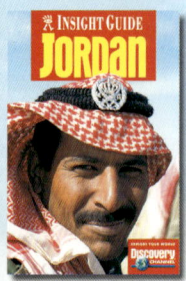

Insight Guides is the award-winning classic series that provides the complete picture of a destination, with expert and informative text and the world's best photography. Each book has everything you need, being an ideal travel planner, a reliable on-the-spot guide, and a superb souvenir of a trip. Nearly 200 titles.

Insight Maps are designed to complement the guidebooks. They provide full, clear mapping of major destinations, list top sights, and their laminated finish makes them durable and easy to fold. More than 100 titles.

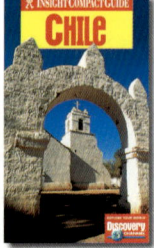

Insight Compact Guides are handy reference books, modestly priced but comprehensive. Text, pictures and maps are all cross-referenced, making them ideal books for on-the-spot use. 120 titles.

Insight Pocket Guides pioneered the concept of the authors as "local hosts" who provide personal recommendations, just as they would give honest advice to a friend. Pull-out map included. 120 titles.

INSIGHT GUIDES

The world's largest collection of visual travel guides